I0216526

IN THE UNLIKELY EVENT OF A WATER LANDING

IN THE UNLIKELY EVENT OF A WATER LANDING

LESSONS FROM LANDING IN THE HUDSON RIVER

ANDREW JAMISON, MD

Healthy Life Press
Orlando, Florida

IN THE UNLIKELY EVENT OF A WATER LANDING

Copyright © 2010, 2013 by Andrew Jamison, MD, and
Healthy Life Press, 2603 Drake Drive, Orlando, FL 32810
www.healthylifepress.com

Cover photo and internal photos of Flight 1549
© Greg Lam Pak Ng - All Rights Reserved.

Printed in the United States of America

All rights reserved. No part of this publication may be repro-
duced, stored in a retrieval system, or transmitted in any form
or by any means - for example, electronic, photocopy, record-
ing - without the prior written permission of the publisher. The
only exception is brief quotations in printed reviews.

Library of Congress Cataloging-in-Publication Data

Jamison, Andrew
  In the Unlikely Event of a Water Landing: Lessons from
  Landing in the Hudson River

ISBN 978-1-9392674-0-5

1. Autobiography; 2. Religious Inspiration

Published by Healthy Life Press. Most Healthy Life Press resources
are available worldwide through bookstores and online outlets, depending on their format. This book also exists in a downloadable
and printable PDF from www.healthylifepress.com. Multiple copy
discounts may be arranged by contacting the publisher at the ad-
dress above, or by e-mailing: info@healthylifepress.com.
Distribution of printed or eBook formatted copies is a violation of
international copyright law, and strictly forbidden.

DEDICATION

To my loving
and
wonderful wife,
Jennifer

FOREWORD

In my years of working on the mission field, with international relief efforts, and now with the 17,000 member Christian Medical & Dental Associations, I've traveled over 2 million miles by air, with certain segments in planes that seemed held together by duct tape, baling twine, and prayer or presumption, or both. While there have been some times when I almost met my Maker, I doubt I've ever seen anything more riveting than that January 15, 2009 photo of US Airways Flight 1549 floating in the icy waters of the Hudson River.

It was amazing to hear that everyone survived, without major injury to either passengers or plane. But my amazement multiplied when I learned that one of our members, Andrew Jamison (then a medical student, now an Intern) had been on that plane, and possibly even in some of the photos I had seen of the passengers deplaning into the life rafts.

Soon after the event, it was my privilege to interview Andrew and his wife, Jennifer, for a recorded program that I knew would bless and inspire our members. Later, this interview served as the basis for an article by Andrew that was published in our journal, *Today's Christian Doctor*.

Now in the form of this book you can keep a copy of Andrew's story in your purse or pocket, briefcase or backpack, to review from time to time, or to give away to someone you believe needs to know what Andrew is trying to say – specifically, that in all things God is sovereign and that, for those who trust Him, this truth is the greatest source of comfort and peace in times of difficulty, however overwhelming they may seem to be.

But before you read on, ask yourself how you would handle being in a disabled plane, screaming toward earth and almost certain death, with only seconds to live. What would you think about? What would you do? Would you be more concerned with trying to preserve your life, or would you think

7

about the passengers around you, some of them about to enter eternity without knowing the Lord?

I've known a number of truly great men and women. They all had one thing in common: character. The United States Air Force Academy defines character as, "The sum of qualities of moral excellence that stimulate a person to do the right thing, which is manifest through right and proper actions despite internal and external pressures to the contrary." Adversity is surely one pressure that gives character a chance to express itself. In fact, the apostle Paul wrote about adversity and how times of testing prove our character and give us, and others, hope.

When you're hurtling toward death the character already developed in you takes over like an auto-pilot, and finds expression in one way or another. In Andrew's case, while others might have screamed in terror, his response was to ask the nearby passengers if he could PRAY with them. Now that's the kind of doctor I want to attend me when things are taking a turn for the worse, or as the saying goes, it seems like the wings are about to fall off.

Andrew would tell you he's not special because he's a doctor, since we're all equally special to God. Nor is he perfect. He's just a follower of Jesus, a person who is still in the process of seeking to become more like his Master, the "Great Physician."

And that's the point in the end. It isn't so much what you do for work, or what you accomplish in life, but who you are and who you are becoming that really matters, and when the chips are down this kind of character will find expression, one way or another.

David Stevens, MD
CEO, Christian Medical & Dental Associations*

*Publisher's note – for information about the Christian Medical & Dental Associations, see the information at back of this book.

INTRODUCTION

Air travel is one of the safest ways to get around the country. There are fewer accidents on major airlines than any other form of transportation. Despite this assurance, there still rests a fear in most people whenever they step on a plane that is not present when using other forms of transportation. The fear is that you might be involved in a plane crash. Rarely does anything go wrong, but when it does go wrong it is usually catastrophic.

On January 15, 2009, I was fortunate to be on the most successful water ditching involving a major airline in aviation history. I was one of 155 passengers and crew on board US Airways Flight 1549 that was supposed to travel from New York City to Charlotte, North Carolina.

Instead of landing in Charlotte, however, this flight landed in the Hudson River. Everyone on board survived. Without doubt, we owe our lives to the sovereignty of God and the expertise of our pilot, Captain Chesley B. "Sully" Sullenberger III.

What follows is my story – not only about what happened and how it affected me then and how it continues to affect me now, but more importantly this is my personal expression of gratitude to the Lord God for keeping me here so I might continue to love and serve Him and my fellow human beings to the best of my ability, for as long as He wants me to stay here and do that.

–Andrew Jamison, MD

THE MATCH

In the middle of our fourth year of medical school, my wife Jennifer and I went through what every medical student hoping to move on with their career goes through. It's called the match process.

There are a lot of details to it, but you basically match up programs and applicants for your particular specialty. The general idea is that you apply to the programs you like for the particular specialty or specialties you are interested in. You apply across the country in hopes of getting an interview. Then you go around the country interviewing at different locations and rank the programs you like best and submit it.

The programs submit their rank lists of applicants as well, and the "computer" spits out where you will spend the next several years of your life and what you'll be doing. The process becomes exponentially more complicated when you try to match as a couple so that your two rank lists are linked. This is so you don't end up in different cities.

On a Thursday in March, the match results are released. Every school does it differently, but where we went to school it was a big ceremony. Friends and family come to watch you open up your letter, which tells you where you are going and what type of residency you matched into.

As you can imagine, this makes for a fairly dramatic process. Some people are brought to tears of joy; others weep tears of disappointment. For many people, this is the culmination of your four years of medical school.

Needless to say this process can be stressful. One thing I didn't mention was the possibility of not matching. This is the real fear. What if after all these years the "computer" doesn't find you a match? This happens more frequently with more competitive specialties such as radiation oncology, anesthesiology, plastic surgery, radiology, and dermatology, which was what I was applying for.

On January 15th, I was at a dermatology interview in the Bronx. It was a about halfway through the interview season and I was in top interview shape. I had a pretty good idea of the questions that were going to be asked, and after several other interviews I had refined my answers. Residency interviews are a little like speed dating. Many of the departments have several faculty members, and it was not unusual to have ten to fifteen interviews in a morning, all about ten minutes long. A bell would ring or someone would knock on the door and you would move to the next interviewer.

This particular day in the Bronx was different though. For whatever reason, I was scheduled for an interview day in which most of the local New York students came to interview. It was abbreviated, I had three interviews, a quick tour, lunch, and I was done.

I was scheduled for a 9:30 PM flight home to Charlotte because as a general rule most interviews went until 4 to 5 PM, but that day I was done by 1 PM. I briefly thought about walking around the city, since I had never been to New York City, but instead I decided to head toward LaGuardia to see if I could get on an earlier flight home.

After much help from a New York City student who had interviewed that day as well, I found my way through the subway system to where it would be much cheaper to catch a cab to LaGuardia.

Even so, by the time I finally arrived at LaGuardia, I was already a little bit frazzled. I approached the US Airways desk and asked if there was any way I could get on an earlier flight. He tapped on the keyboard for awhile and informed me that I could, but it would cost an extra $50. For most people, I imagine, it would be well worth $50 to avoid spending eight hours in LaGuardia airport, but based on where we were financially, that just couldn't happen.

Jennifer and I had been living off of student loans that we originally applied for when we had done our budget for the year the previous June. This money had to hold us over until we made our first checks in some unknown residency program, probably in August of 2009. We had planned on cashing in some stocks that I had bought back in high school, but they hadn't been doing very well over the past year. Unfortunately, for a lot of people including myself, during the fall the banking crisis hit its peak and the stock market plummeted. So here we are trying to interview on about half the money we had originally budgeted for, and trying to hold out as long as we could. So I just couldn't justify the $50.

As I walked away from the counter, the agent said, "Let me try one more thing." He tapped away again and said that there was a flight leaving in a few minutes and that he could get me on standby. There looked like there might be one seat left, but I would have to run to catch it.

I took off toward the gate and experienced my first miracle of that day. There was no one waiting in the security line. As a result, I was able to get through security in less than two minutes and was on my way. I made it to the gate and there were still people waiting to board. I walked up to the counter, checked in, and got a ticket, seat 25 E.

Before I boarded, I sent a text message to Jennifer telling her I had gotten on an earlier flight that was about to leave. Then I called my parents, who were supposed to pick me up in Charlotte, and let them know I was on Flight 1549, and that I should be able to get home in time for dinner.

U·S AIRWAYS

Name of Passenger

JAMSION/RICHARD

CONF: ABFZG1/US   ZONE 3

FFD:

NEW YORK LAGUARDIA

CHARLOTTE

Flight	DEPARTS	Date
1549	245P	15JAN

Gate	Boarding Time	Seat
21	215P	25E

On The Taxiway

It had been a crazy day already, I was still in my suit from the interviews, which I had made a point to try and change out of as soon as I could on most interview days, but today had just been too busy. I found my seat in the back of the plane, one row from the back lavatory, in between two strangers I would get to know much better in a few minutes.

As I took my seat, I pulled out two books I had been reading on the interview trail. One, *The Sovereignty of God*, by Arthur W. Pink, was a heavy theological book that had been convincing me of just how sovereign God is. The other was a little lighter read, *Prince Caspian*, by CS Lewis. This is a children's book with great biblical allegories.

After my already long day I was more in the mood for the children's book, so I picked up *Prince Caspian* and finally began to relax. I remember sitting for quite some time on the taxiway waiting our turn to takeoff, as I continued to read my book and think about the interview questions earlier that day and how I could have answered them differently. I looked back through the details of the dermatology program and began to mentally rank it in my head compared to the other programs I had interviewed at.

During this time on the taxiway, the flight attendants went through their typical speech of what to do if... "In the unlikely event of a water landing, your seat cushion may be used as a flotation device." I only half-way registered what she said, but I guarantee you, those words will never fly past my brain again, unattended.

I halfway listened and kept reading my book.

BIRD STRIKE

The take off was uneventful and I continued to read my book, waiting for the announcement that it was all right to use electronics. About that time I heard a loud thud and the plane jerked a little bit. There are certain noises on an airplane you really don't want to hear, and this qualified as one of them. Nevertheless, things like this happened quite often when going through turbulence and such. I had heard funny noises on planes many times before and my safety check had always been to look at the flight attendants. If they weren't worried, I wasn't worried . . . and I'd go back to my business. This time it was different. I looked at the flight attendant, and she was definitely not all right with that noise.

About this time someone a few rows ahead of me said they could see the engine sparking and a peculiar smell began to fill the cabin. At the time, I couldn't place that smell other than it was smokey. I've subsequently heard several other people who were on the plane describe it as a smell of burnt turkey, which after the fact was a perfect description. The flight attendant behind me in the back of the cabin was reaching for something between the last seat and the lavatory. It looked like a large radio of some type. That's when things began to get a little more real. This was not standard operating procedure. I had never seen this thing before.

The plane was beginning to descend noticeably at this point. A few weeks earlier, at another interview dinner, I had had a conversation with a young commercial airline pilot just out of school. He was the husband of one the applicants. Any time I get to talk with a pilot I always ask him about his closest call. My older brother is a fighter pilot in the Navy. I often live vicariously through him as he tells the most interesting stories about his close calls.

The young pilot had told me how, when he was flying with his trainer, one of the engines had lost power. He said it wasn't that scary, his training just kicked in and he went through his checklists of restarting the engines and eventually the engine restarted. "Besides that," he said, "most planes are designed so that they can fly on just one engine in the event that they lose the other." Being used to my brother's stories, I wasn't too impressed at the time. However, now with Flight 1549 obviously in trouble, that young pilot's story became very real. I felt like I had a pretty good idea of what was going on in the cockpit.

This provided some comfort, initially. But that was because I was operating on the supposition that we had blown the right engine. I was a little concerned that the plane might catch fire, but other than that I thought we would be okay.

After the first few frenzied seconds of the flight attendant grabbing the transponder, things calmed down and it was quiet. That's when the quietness of the moment hit me like a punch in the gut. It was way too quiet. There was no engine noise.

None.

I thought to myself, *We haven't just lost the right engine, we have no engines.*

I later found out that people on the left side of the plane had a similar experience of thinking they had just lost the left engine, until they heard that eerie silence as well. It is a surreal experience to be thousands of feet in the air in an airplane with no background engine noise as the plane steadily descended.

We banked to the left, and as I looked out the left window, there below us was Manhattan. I knew enough to know that there was no way we were getting back to LaGuardia through Manhattan. I didn't know a whole lot about New York City other than it was really crowded with busy interstates and so there were probably no good places to land. Admittedly, the Hudson River never crossed my mind as an option.

As the realization of what was most certainly about to happen sank in, the most interesting things began to cross my mind. My first thought was to call Jennifer. I pulled out my phone and then paused, wondering: *What am I going to say? The plane is about to crash. I'm going to die. I love you. It's ok to remarry. I'm sorry I procrastinated getting life insurance.* (Ironically, two months earlier we had had a serious discussion about getting life insurance while I was still young and healthy and could get a good premium.)

I knew I would only reach her voice mail, since she was in clinic, so then it hit me that I would be leaving this terrible message that might haunt her for the rest of her life. I didn't know which would be worse – to have this voice mail on her phone, or for her to hear about the crash gradually through the media? In the end, it didn't matter. My phone wouldn't turn on.

I think God didn't allow my phone to turn on because at that moment, Jennifer was not the person I was supposed to be talking to. It was one of those "duh" moments. *I should probably pray about what is about to happen*, I thought. *And maybe I should include the passengers around me.*

In the hospital if you want to pray with someone, you better ask if it's ok with them first. Otherwise, that is a good way to get fired. This had been beat into my brain to the point where I had not taken advantage of prayer in the hospital nearly enough. Regardless, I sheepishly asked the lady beside me if it would be ok if I said a prayer for us.

I didn't know where the people around me stood with God at that moment, if they had believed before this moment in God or Jesus. But it honestly didn't matter at this point.

I've heard it said there are no atheists in foxholes. I think this holds true for passengers in an imminent plane crash as well, though there aren't too many of them to ask about it.

It never occurred to me to pray for the plane not to crash. In my mind that was a done deal, we were about to crash and everyone was about to die.

I don't remember exactly what I said, but it probably went something like this, "Lord, I pray for your peace to protect our hearts and minds. And Lord, if there is anyone on this plane who has never trusted You as Lord and Savior, I pray that in this crazy moment they will put their soul in Your hands. And Lord, God, I affirm Your sovereignty over all things, including what is about to happen to us. Hard as it is to imagine, I know that You will bring good from it in the end. Amen."

What happened next was the greatest miracle of that day to me. I wish I could describe the peace that I experienced on that plane. It is beyond explanation and everything logical that I know of. I have never been more at peace in my life. It was the greatest feeling I had ever felt.

Everything from my medical training tells me I should have been revved up, ready to do anything I could to stay alive. My adrenals (the little glands that sit above both our kidneys, producing epinephrine and other excitatory hormones) should have been secreting more endorphins into my blood stream than I had ever experienced.

But instead, I was calm, relaxed, and in a state of complete peace. The only way I know how to explain it comes from a passage in Philippians, where we are told not to be anxious about anything, but in everything by prayer and petition to present our requests to God and the peace of God, which surpasses all understanding, will guard our hearts and minds in Christ Jesus. I believe that in that most desperate of desperate situations, God granted me His peace and it was amazing.

The next thing I remember, the Captain (Captain Sullenberger) made his first and only announcement over the PA system. I'll never forget his words. In the calmest, most monotone voice, as though he was announcing what the weather was in Charlotte he said, "Brace the cabin for impact."

If there was ever a doubt about what was happening, it was immediately cleared up from that point on. The flight attendants kept saying over and over to cover our heads, fasten our seat belts, and we all assumed the universal crash position.

It seemed like an eternity from the announcement to the time we actually made impact. After the announcement, there was no more talking, just the faint sound of a few people sobbing and a young child crying. I closed my eyes, and even in that moment was covered with that unexplainable peace. Thoughts of heaven and what that would be like ran through my mind.

IMPACT

Probably the most frequent question I am asked about the incident was what the impact was like. My answer has pretty much always been the same, "I don't know. When you're expecting to get ripped to pieces, anything short of that is pretty good."

The best way I know how to explain it, is that it was like a water park ride. When I was in high school, I worked three summers at an amusement park. At the end of a hot day some us would go on "The Grand Rapids." I think most amusement parks have a ride like this. You sit in a large barge-like boat with a few other people. You go up this roller coaster type ramp, then you float around the corner to this big drop off.

Then you go flying down this hill into this large body of water and make a great splash. When you hit the bottom you get jarred a little bit, and this great wave of water flies out to soak the people watching from the observation deck. Then you just float on to where you get off the ride. It happens quick and then you are done.

It was very similar to this ride, however, as we continued to go through the water, you could feel the plane beginning to fish tail a little bit to the left. *This is it*, I told myself. *Here comes the flipping*.

But the plane never flipped. It just came to a stop.

THE WATER

Almost immediately after impact I felt a cold rush of water at my feet. By the time we came to a stop, the water had reached my knees. As soon as the plane stopped, everyone stood up and looked toward the exit doors. My closest exit was in the rear.

I looked back and there was the flight attendant, up to her chest in water saying, "We can't go out the back. We can't go out the back!" Within a matter of seconds the water had gone from my ankles to my knees, and I was thinking that soon we were all going to be immersed in ice cold water.

In looking at photographs of the accident, it's easy to see what happened. The plane was tilted toward its tail so there was water in the back of the plane almost to the ceiling and the front of the plane was dry. That didn't process for me initially. I thought the whole plane was going down that quick, and now a new fear seized me.

I am going to drown.

There have been times in my life where I have studied hard to learn certain medical knowledge only to later wish I could somehow forget what I've learned. This was one of those times where I probably knew too much about drowning to be of any comfort to myself or anyone else.

Drowning is an interesting phenomenon. As mammals, we can't take oxygen from water, instead if our lungs fill with fluid we asphyxiate. This isn't as straightforward as you might think, though. Naturally, you hold your breath for as long as possible, but as carbon dioxide builds up in your blood your drive to breathe grows stronger and stronger.

Eventually, you reach a breath-hold break point where

you inhale water. This is only the beginning, though. You then go into laryngospasm where your vocal cords clamp down, keeping water out of your lungs and diverting them to your stomach. If you haven't lost consciousness up to this point, you soon do, since if water isn't getting to your lungs neither is oxygen. Even while unconscious, the reflex is so strong to keep water out of your lungs, you still have laryngospasm. This eventually relaxes, and you are overwhelmed with water in your lungs, and you asphyxiate.

This was the worst part of the entire experience. I went from complete peace to absolute fear. I looked frantically up at the ceiling for some type of escape. I looked at the window to see if I could somehow bust it out. These were obviously hopeless thoughts. I could feel my throat beginning to tighten already.

The exit doors in the front of the cabin had opened up and people were heading *en masse* up the aisle and over the seats toward them. There was a large crowd around the exits to the wings. Someone was directing the passengers, and asking them to keep coming forward to the front exits.

I don't remember much about the exit itself. I don't know how long it took, but I bet we set a record for the world's fastest deplaning.

I remember being about half way up the aisle and the words of the flight attendant came back to mind, "In the unlikely event of a water landing, your seat may be used as a flotation device." In my panic of just wanting to get out of the rear of the plane, I had forgotten to take my seat with me. I frantically looked around for other seats I could take, but from where I was at on to the front they were all taken, and I wasn't about to turn back around and get mine.

Fortunately, as I neared the front exit the co-captain was handing out life jackets. Then the captain walked past me to make sure everyone was out.

I exited out of what would have been the normal exit everyone would have taken had we landed in Charlotte like my ticket stub said we would. I slid a few feet down to the raft/slide that was floating in the Hudson river. Shortly after I slid down, the co-captain and then the captain joined us in our raft.

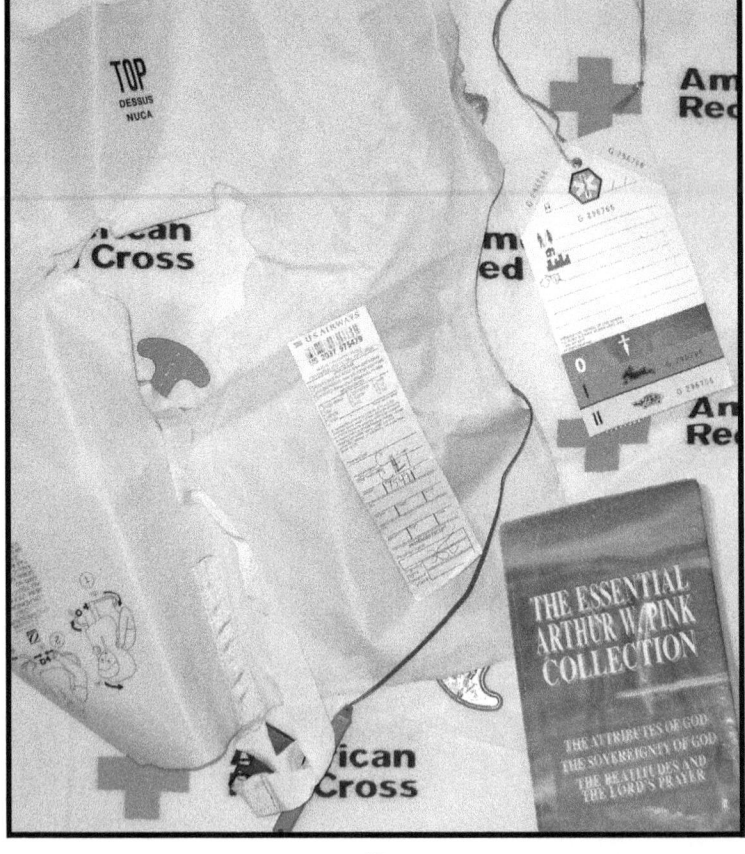

THE RAFT AND HOME

At this point I felt pretty good, and I think most people on the raft would say the same thing. I didn't care how cold it was. I didn't care that I was standing in ankle deep water. I was out of that plane and we were going to be all right. The co-captain looked at the captain and congratulated him on the most successful ditching in airline history. He said that a few minutes earlier he had felt certain that they were going to be pulling parts of themselves out of the instrument panel.

At that moment, the impact of just what had happened hit me. We should not have made it out of this as well as we did. Since the plane was just sitting there, with us tethered to it, I asked probably the dumbest question I could have asked, of Captain Sullenberger. "I didn't know the river was so shallow here," I said.

"The plane is actually still floating," he replied. "And we need to cut ourselves free, before it sinks and takes us with it."

By this time, ferries had come from what seemed like every direction. From somewhere on one of the ferries, a pocket knife was thrown our way so we could cut ourselves free. We then proceeded to help all of the women out of the raft, and onto the ferry first.

When I had made it onto the raft, I had reached into my pocket and pulled out my cell phone that had earlier not turned on. This time the phone came on without any trouble. My first thought was to call Jennifer. The call went straight to her voice mail as I had suspected it would have earlier. In an effort to try and nip things in the bud I left the following message. "Hey babe, the plane just crashed but I'm okay.

We're in the river right now. I'll call you when I get a chance. Love you." I would later learn that it would have been much better to let her know that I was *in a raft* in the river, not just in the river.

Back in Charleston, South Carolina, where Jennifer was in clinic, she had finished up early and was heading home. While in clinic she had put her phone on silent, so she had missed the numerous text messages and phone calls that had come her way over the past thirty minutes. She checked her text messages first and read my message that I had got on the earlier flight 1549 home and while reading this message got a phone call from her father.

The first thing he asked was what flight I was on and after just reading the text message this was an easy answer to come up with. He then informed her that there had been a plane crash and that I was most likely on that plane. He went on to say that they thought everyone had survived the crash, but that it was very cold and the main concern was hypothermia.

As she was hearing all of this, she lost the connection which always happened when walking between the two hospital buildings at MUSC. Instead of panicking, she said a quick prayer and saw that she had several voice mails, the first of which being my voice mail telling her that I was OK, but in the river. We joke about it now, but she had this mental image of me floating down the river with my cell phone to my ear.

Once on the ferry, it was an interesting and somewhat exciting time. It was a good feeling to be alive. I called Jennifer again and this time she answered. Apparently, I just kept repeating how great our God is and hung up. As the excitement began to wear off, the coldness also started to come on. We had been in the water only ten minutes or so thanks to the fast response of the NYC ferry captains and the first responders, but the water was nearly at freezing that day.

The goal once aboard the ferry became to try and warm up. The ferry was heated, so I tried to find where the heating ducts came out and stayed close once I found them. The ferry took us to where we were triaged, and those who were injured were taken to the hospital. The rest of us stayed in the warmth of the port waiting on what would happen next. This process took quite some time, but eventually we were all taken by buses to the Crowne Plaza where the US Airways representatives were waiting for us.

Flight 1549 had been scheduled to take off at 2:45, it was now closer to 7:30, and I happened to know there was another flight leaving LaGuardia going to Charlotte at 9, since that was my originally ticketed flight. My only request was to somehow get on that plane and get home. There was a handful of us who felt the same way. We just wanted to get home and we knew that taking another airplane was the fastest way to do it.

It was an interesting flight back home. They took us by bus back to the airport. We were escorted through security quickly. They really didn't have to check anything, since all of our luggage, including our carry ons were sitting in the Hudson River. Then they gave us the choice of any seat on the airplane, which was one of the smaller jets without a first class. To no one's surprise, we all huddled around the exit row.

I think, overall, it was a good thing to be back on another airplane right after everything happened. I was still unsure how big this whole thing was going to be; I doubt that anyone involved knew it would be the story it turned out to be. I remember sitting on the plane back home and thinking to myself, *I just survived a plane crash and it wasn't that bad, and now I'm on another plane finally going home.* It had been a long day, for sure. I slept most of the way home.

THE SHORT-TERM EFFECTS

One of the most surprising aspects of the story has been the amount of media coverage it has received. I knew this was a big deal when it happened, but I could have never imagined the barrage of media coverage that followed almost immediately. Everyone wanted to hear the story.

When I arrived in Charlotte, the US Airways officials met us at the gate and offered to take us out of the back of the airport so we could avoid the media if we wanted to.

I didn't think much of it and elected to go through the terminal like anybody else would. I had already arranged to meet Jennifer and my parents, who had driven by now to Charlotte, at Baggage Claim C.

As I went down the escalators on the other side of security, I was surprised to find a mass of cameras and microphones waiting at the bottom of the stairs. I certainly didn't expect the amount of media that would end up being there. It was pretty easy to tell who had been on Flight 1549. We didn't have any luggage. We were wearing these white socks that the Red Cross had given us, as well as a Red Cross blanket.

I was still holding tight to my life jacket that co-captain Skiles had given me. They asked for interviews. "I just want to find my wife," I said. When I finally found Jennifer, the cameras and the lights no longer mattered as we embraced each other.

Then from behind me I heard a voice say, "That would be a good one." Almost immediately, the crowd of cameras grew as they followed me through the baggage claim area.

As I was getting into the car to go home, a CNN reporter asked me what I thought about the pilot. I responded saying that, "God was certainly looking out after all of us."

This brought about a response, mostly on the Internet, that I would have never expected. The event was dubbed "Miracle on the Hudson," and a few atheist blog sites responded sharply, making me the subject of much ridicule with my previously mentioned comments. I couldn't believe some of the hateful things that were said, and I wanted to blast back with some theological, apologetic responses.

For example, I might have said: "Yes, God brought the geese, too. No sparrow falls to the ground without Him knowing about it. But that doesn't change that He brought that plane down safely, too." In the end, I decided that replying this way, or in any way at all, to people with such obvious hatred for God and His way, would just keep the online fires fueled, so I did not respond.

I was fully convinced of the sovereignty of God in this entire event, and I let everyone know it. However, a short time later, the strong feelings I had about the sovereignty of God, which had carried me through the crash and afterward, would face their strongest challenge in my mind.

Less than two weeks later, everything I had wanted to say would come into question when a plane crashed going from New York to Buffalo, killing everyone on board. I remember watching the news coverage of this crash and thinking, *Why wasn't that me? Why did God in all of His sovereignty save flight 1549, but not this flight?*

I was faced with the most difficult question that comes up when you talk about the sovereignty of God. If God is sovereign why do bad things still happen? I had wrestled with this question before and was always reassured on an intellectual level with theological answers involving glorifying God to some degree, and how as humans it is impossible to know what God is using to accomplish that purpose.

There have been many books and much discussion about this topic, and in the past I had always accepted it at face value, on faith: God is sovereign and in control of everything, and yet bad things still happen. He does not delight in them, but He is able to redeem them for good.

Although this argument can be presented extremely well from a theological perspective, when you are actually living it, somehow everything that you took at face value in the past can get called into question.

I had to go back and reevaluate exactly what I believed. And this time I could not accept it just because some well-respected pastor had told me it was true. I had to wrestle with God, personally, over these issues in order to resolve them for myself, now that the questions had become personalized.

I read a systematic theology textbook on God's providence, and prayed long and hard over this issue. I went back and read over and over the Scriptures on God's sovereignty. Ultimately, it came down to two questions in my mind. *Do I believe the Scriptures to be true when they speak of God's sovereignty; and, do I believe that God is a loving God?*

In other words, in the end, though the issues were logical and theological, it came down to faith. Thankfully, God granted me this faith and reaffirmed my previously held beliefs, and He has used this experience to strengthen my faith.

Another question that kept running through my mind was: *What am I doing with my life now? If God had just saved me from what I thought was imminent death, He must have some great plan for my life. This must represent some changing point in my life.*

Then I would correct myself: *God has always had a plan for me, and this crash doesn't change that necessarily. The turning point in my life wasn't this plane crash, but the day I accepted Christ as my Savior.*

Through my Christian walk, God had certainly gotten my attention in different ways, but the path was still mostly all the same. What the crash did do was lead to a reassessment of my life and what I was currently doing. This was especially true since the event came right during match season. I kept asking myself if dermatology was what God was calling me to practice as a specialty. Once again, this was a very reaffirming process that made me more sure of where I was in life.

Probably the most tangible and immediate effect I felt was peace during the matching process. Jennifer and I were going through a very difficult couples match, with most of the odds stacked against us being able to find what we both hoped for, in the same location.

I had not done all of the things that most of the applicants had done. I had not done any research while in medical school and I had not done any away rotations. During the summer before our fourth year, when you typically do rotations, Jennifer had been stuck with a pair of bloody scissors, while on a mission trip in Africa. I could not justify applying for away rotations that would take me away from Jennifer for four weeks at a time when we didn't know if she would end up seroconverting to HIV positive. A year of blood testing later, thankfully, Jennifer is HIV negative.

I had carried the burden of the match throughout interview season depending upon everything I had done during medical school and my interviewing skills to get me a spot, and compensate for my otherwise weak application. Two days after the crash I was on another plane heading to another dermatology interview. Everything seemed to revolve around these interviews, which had become a full-time job that even a plane crash could not slow down.

The difference after the crash, however, was this great peace that I now had, that my God is big, really really big, and He is faithful. In all honesty, it wasn't even a peace that we would match, it was a peace that God is in control and if we didn't match God had something better in store. After all, He did have a plan for my life and my life had not come to an end on January 15, 2009, so there must be more still to do.

Ultimately, we did match in Temple, Texas, at Scott and White, with programs that were perfectly suited to both of us. The more involved we get in our programs the more we see the hand of God, who led us to His perfect place for us.

Immediately after the crash, I had a range of emotions and feelings. Maybe the most overwhelming was that I should actually be feeling more things. One of the greatest miracles of this event has been the psychological shielding Christ has given me. The night after the crash, I had one of the best nights of sleep I have ever had. To date, I have never had a nightmare or even any dreams about the plane crash.

During the first few months after the crash, I often would think about it, mainly about all of the different scenarios that could have played out and what I would have done. Chances are I will never be in another plane crash, but rest assured that if I am I have replayed every scenario possible in my head and will be prepared.

Another blessing that God brought about through this event was the closeness that my wife and I experienced after it. We feel like we have gone through a lot of things together since we have been married. Third year of medical school was a very difficult time for both us having to deal with the pressures of the hospital for the first time. Then there was the HIV scare during our fourth year, which I mentioned already. Those pressures have been eclipsed by the added stress of us both being interns as I write this.

Through all of these trials, God has seemed to draw us closer to Himself, and in turn closer to each other. I feel like we share a closeness that we would never have felt had it not been for the trials that we have endured together. With each of these trials it has been amazing to see how God has used them to prepare us with what we would face next.

Each time we went through a difficult time I would wonder how anything good could come from it. Then, months or years later, I could see how that situation had perfectly prepared me for what was next.

With that in mind, it is a little bit scary to think of what God may be preparing us for with this experience. Regardless, I am convinced that God does not put us in situations that He will not lead us through. Often in those difficult times I have found a closeness to God that I might not have experienced otherwise.

HOW HAS IT CHANGED ME, LONG-TERM?

During the ride down, one of the greatest feelings was the assurance of salvation I had. I had gone through a period in high school when I really wrestled with the reality of God and if He really existed, or did religion exist as a crutch for those who couldn't deal with the problem of death.

God eventually showed me that He was real, through a slow and gradual process, but the question of God's existence seems to be an arrow Satan has especially for me. When I go through lows in my spiritual walk this is the arrow Satan sends my way.

One of my greatest fears in dealing with this has been that when I'm lying on my deathbed one day, will I doubt the reality of Christ in that crucial moment? How scary that moment would be, if I doubted my Savior then!

Any such thoughts were far from my mind as I was faced with what I thought was certain death. Never had I experienced the reality and closeness with Christ that I experienced in that cabin as we were going down. I long for that feeling daily, but having experienced it once before, I now hold on to a much stronger assurance of my salvation. That may be one of the greatest things that has become central in my walk with Christ since the crash, the assurance of my salvation. This assurance is not because I deserve it, but because He died and rose again to stamp as everlasting Truth His own words, "I give them eternal life, and they shall never perish; no one can snatch them out of my hand. My Father, who has given them to me, is greater than all; no one can snatch them out of my Father's hand. I and the Father are one" (John 10: 28-30, NIV).

In the months after the crash, I began to see that this event could take over my life. Being a survivor could easily become my identity. People might come to see me as that guy who was on that plane. It was a great story and people seemed to like listening to it.

Interestingly, when we moved to Texas, no one knew that I had been on Flight 1549. I had to decide how often I let that information out. Selfishly, part of me enjoyed the notoriety of it. Yet another part of me hated having to tell it and talk about it any more. Both of these were selfish reasons. Then there was this part of me that felt that I should tell the story as often as I could, since it was such a God-glorifying story – at least the account I should be giving of it was.

I have been involved in some type of student ministry for the past eight years, and always the most difficult part of it has been transitioning from ordinary conversation to important spiritual issues. I now had a great way into deep and spiritual matters, with anyone who would listen. Everyone wanted to hear the story, and it became an automatic opening to share the ultimate value of authentic faith. This has been one of the greatest blessings in the whole process, the gift of having this story to tell.

The accident has also served to vividly show me flaws in my character and faith. During the ride down, I had an amazing peace. I had no control over the situation; I wasn't the one in the cockpit. After we landed in the river and the water flooded in up to my knees, the fear of drowning in that icy cold water took over. Water was coming in and I was stuck in this plane and couldn't get out. Both were helpless situations, but this time I felt like there might be something I could do. I could possibly hold my breath long enough to swim to the back exit, or maybe I could kick out a window.

None of these ideas would have worked, but at least they would give me an opportunity to do something to try and save myself. This was the most terrifying part of the whole experience, because I was relying once again upon my abilities to get out of the situation.

I went from one moment of completely relying upon God, while in the next breath God was the furthest thought from my mind. I had done this throughout much of my Christian life. I would give God the big stuff that I couldn't control, but I would hold on to the other stuff that I thought I could influence.

Yet in relying on my own abilities for the things I thought I could manage, even the small stuff could become just as nerve racking as big things. While I was on that plane, God began to do a work in me to give Him even the small things, and He continues to teach me more and more about this.

I'm not really sure what else this experience will change in my life. Immediately after the crash, I felt like it should have changed more. No major decisions changed. But certain changes have happened slowly over time. A year after the crash, I am surprised just how much it has changed my approach to my little day to day matters and decisions, because now I can rest in the peace and knowledge of God's sovereignty.

I hope those who have lost love ones in Christ will be encouraged by knowing the peace that God granted me in such a hopeless time. Had I perished that day, I know that my loved ones would have grieved not only over my death but the manner in which I died. What they would have never known was that the moments before I died were the most peaceful moments I had ever experienced.

Resources from Healthy Life Press

Unless otherwise noted on the site itself, shipping is free for all products purchased through www.healthylifepress.com.

We've Got Mail: The New Testament Letters in Modern English – As Relevant Today as Ever! by Rev. Warren C. Biebel, Jr. – A modern English paraphrase of the New Testament Letters, sure to inspire in readers a loving appreciation for God's Word. (Printed book: $9.95; PDF eBook: $6.95; together: $15.00; commercial eBook reader version: $9.99.)

Hearth & Home – Recipes for Life, by Karey Swan (7th Edition) – Far more than a cookbook, this classic is a life book, with recipes for life as well as for great food. Karey describes how to buy and prepare from scratch a wide variety of tantalizing dishes, while weaving into  the book's fabric the wisdom of the ages plus the recipe that she and her husband used to raise their kids. A great gift for Christmas or for a new bride. (Perfect Bound Version (8 x 10, glossy cover): $17.95; PDF eBook version: $12.95; Together as set: $24.95; commercial eBook reader version: $9.99.)

Who Me, Pray? Prayer 101: Praying Aloud, for Beginners, by Gary A. Burlingame – *Who Me, Pray?* is a practical guide for prayer, based on Jesus' direction in "The Lord's Prayer," with examples provided for use in typical situations where you might be asked or expected to pray in public. (Printed book: $6.95 PDF eBook: $2.99; together: $7.95.)

The Big Black Book – What the Christmas Tree Saw, by Rev. Warren C. Biebel, Jr – An original Christmas story, from the perspective of the Christmas tree. This little book is especially suitable for parents to read to their children at Christmas time or all year-round. (Printed book: $7.95; PDF eBook:

$4.95; Together: $10.95; commercial eBook reader version: $6.95.)

My Broken Heart Sings, the poetry of Gary Burlingame – In 1987, Gary and his wife Debbie lost their son Christopher John, at only six months of age, to a chronic lung disease. This life-changing experience gave them a special heart for helping others through similar loss and pain. (Printed book: $10.95; PDF eBook: $6.95; Together: $13.95; commercial eBook reader version: $9.99 at eChristian.com; Amazon.com; bn.com.)

After Normal: One Teen's Journey Following Her Brother's Death, by Diane Aggen – Based on a journal the author kept following her younger brother's death. It offers helpful insights and understanding for teens facing a similar loss or for those who might wish to understand and help teens facing a similar loss. (Printed book: $11.95; PDF eBook: $6.95; together: $15.00; commercial eBook reader version: $8.99.)

In the Unlikely Event of a Water Landing – Lessons Learned from Landing in the Hudson River, by Andrew Jamison, MD. The author was flying standby on US Airways Flight 1549 toward Charlotte on January 15, 2009, from New York City, where he had been interviewing for a residency position. Little did he know

that the next stop would be the Hudson River. Riveting and inspirational, this book would be especially helpful for people in need of hope and encouragement. (Printed book: $8.95; PDF eBook: $6.95; Together: $12.95; commercial eBook reader version: $8.99.)

Finding Martians in the Dark – Everything I Needed to Know About Teaching Took Me Only 30 Years to Learn, by Dan M. Biebel – Packed with wise advice based on hard experience, and laced with humor, this book is a perfect teacher's gift year-round. Susan J. Wegmann, PhD, says, "Biebel's sardonic wit is mellowed by a genuine love for kids and teaching. . . . A Whitman-like sensibility flows through his stories of teaching, learning, and life." (Printed book: $10.95; PDF eBook: $6.95; Together: $15.00; commercial eBook: $9.99.)

Because We're Family and *Because We're Friends*, by Gary A. Burlingame – Sometimes things related to faith can be hard to discuss with your family and friends. These booklets

are designed to be given as gifts, to help you open the door to discussing spiritual matters with family members and friends who are open to such a conversation. (Printed book: $5.95 each; PDF eBook: $4.95 each; together: $9.95 per pair [printed & eBook of the same title]; commercial eBook reader version: $5.95.)

The Transforming Power of Story: How Telling Your Story Brings Hope to Others and Healing to Yourself, by Elaine Leong Eng, MD, and David B.

Biebel, DMin – This book demonstrates, through multiple true life stories, how sharing one's story, especially in a group setting, can bring hope to listeners and healing to the one who shares. Individuals facing difficulties will find this book greatly encouraging. (Printed book: $14.99; PDF eBook: $9.99; together: $19.99; commercial eBook reader version: $9.99.)

PLEASE NOTE: Prices of resources listed in this catalog may have changed since these pages were printed. Current prices are available at: www.healthylifepress.com. *Unless otherwise noted on the site itself, shipping is free for all products purchased through www.healthylifepress.com.*

You Deserved a Better Father: Good Parenting Takes a Plan, by Robb Brandt, MD – About parenting by intention, and other lessons the author learned through the loss of his firstborn son. It is especially for parents who believe that bits and pieces of leftover time will be enough for their own children. (Printed book: $12.95 each; PDF eBook: $6.95; together: $17.95; commercial eBook reader version: $9.99.)

Jonathan, You Left Too Soon, by David B. Biebel, DMin

One pastor's journey through the loss of his son, into the darkness of depression, and back into the light of joy again, emerging with a renewed sense of mission. (Printed book: $12.95; PDF eBook: $5.99; together: $15.00 at healthylifepress.com.

The Spiritual Fitness Checkup for the 50-Something Woman, by Sharon V. King, PhD – Following the stages of a routine medical exam, the author describes ten spiritual fitness "checkups" midlife women can conduct to assess their spiritual health and tone up their relationship with God. Each checkup consists of the author's personal reflections, a Scripture reference for meditation, and a "Spiritual Pulse Check," with exercises readers can use for personal application. (Printed book: $8.95; PDF eBook: $6.95; together: $12.95.)

 *The Other Side of Life – Over 60? God Still Has a Plan for You*, by Rev. Warren C. Biebel Jr. – Drawing on biblical examples and his 60-plus years of pastoral experience, Rev. Biebel helps older (and younger) adults understand God's view of aging and the rich life available to everyone who seeks a deeper relationship with God as they age. Rev. Biebel explains how to: Identify God's ongoing plan for your life; Rely on faith to manage the anxieties of aging; Form positive, supportive relationships; Cultivate patience; Cope with new technologies; Develop spiritual integrity; Understand the effects of dementia; Develop a Christ-centered perspective of aging. (Printed book: $10.95; PDF eBook: $6.95; together: $15.00; commercial eBook reader version: $9.99.)

My Faith, My Poetry by Gary A. Burlingame – This unique book of Christian poetry is actually two in one. The first collection of poems, *A Day in the Life*, explores a working parent's daily journey of faith. The reader is carried from morning to bedtime, from "In the Details," to "I Forgot to Pray,"  back to "Home Base," and finally to "Eternal Love Divine." The second collection of poems, *Come Running*, is wonder, joy, and faith wrapped up in words that encourage and inspire the mind and the heart. (Printed book: $10.95; PDF eBook: $6.95; together: $13.95; commercial eBook reader version: $9.99.)

On Eagles' Wings, by Sara Eggleston – One woman's life journey from idyllic through chaotic to joy, carried all the way by the One who has promised to never leave us nor forsake us. Remarkable, poignant, moving, and inspiring, this autobiographical account will help many who are facing difficulties that seem too great to overcome or even bear at all. It is proof that Isaiah 40:31 is as true today as when it was penned, "But they that wait upon the LORD shall renew their strength; they shall mount up with wings as eagles; they shall run, and not be weary; and they shall walk, and not faint." (Printed book: $14.95; PDF eBook: $8.95; together: $22.95; commercial eBook reader version: $9.99.)

Richer Descriptions, by Gary A. Burlingame – A unique and handy manual, covering all <u>nine</u> human senses in seven chapters, for Christian speakers and writers. Exercises and a speaker's checklist equip speakers to engage their audiences in a richer experience. Writing examples and a writer's guide help  writers bring more life to the characters and scenes of their stories. Bible references encourage a deeper appreciation of being created by God for a sensory existence. (Printed book: $15.95; PDF eBook: $8.95; together: $22.95; commercial eBook reader version: $9.99.)

Unless otherwise noted on the site itself, shipping is free for all products purchased through <u>www.healthylifepress.com</u>.

Treasuring Grace, by Rob Plumley and Tracy Roberts – *This novel was inspired by a dream.* Liz Swanson's life isn't quite what she'd imagined, but she considers herself lucky. She has a good husband, beautiful children, and fulfillment outside of her home through volunteer work. On some days she doesn't even notice the dull ache in her heart. While she's preparing for their summer kickoff at Lake George, the ache disappears and her sudden happiness is mistaken for anticipation of their weekend. However, as the family heads north, there are clouds on the horizon that have nothing to do with the weather. Only Liz's daughter, who's found some of her mother's hidden journals, has any idea what's wrong. But by the end of the weekend, there will be no escaping the truth or its painful buried secrets. Printed: $12.95; PDF eBook: $7.95; together: $19.95; commercial eBook reader version: $9.99.

Life's A Symphony, by Mary Z. Smith – When Kate Spence Cooper receives the news that her husband, Jack, has been killed in the war, she and her young son Jeremy move back to Crawford Wood, Tennessee to be closer to family. Since Jack's death Kate feels that she's lost trust in everyone, including God. Will she

ever find her way back to the only One whom she can always depend upon? And what about Kate's match making brother, Chance? The cheeky man has other ideas on how to bring happiness into his sister's life once more. (Printed book: $12.95; PDF eBook: $7.95; together: $19.95; commercial eBook reader version: $9.99.)

Your Mind at Its Best – 40 Ways To Keep Your Brain Sharp by David B. Biebel, DMin; James E. Dill, MD; and, Bobbie Dill, RN – Everyone wants their mind to function at high levels throughout life. In 40 easy-to-understand chapters, readers will discover a wide variety of tips and tricks to keep their minds sharp. Synthesizing science and self-help, *Your Mind at Its Best* makes fascinating neurological discoveries understandable and immediately applicable to readers of any age. (Printed book: $13.99.)

From Orphan to Physician – The Winding Path, by Chun-Wai Chan, MD – From the foreword: "In this book, Dr. Chan describes how his family escaped to Hong Kong, how they survived in utter poverty, and how he went from being an orphan to graduating from Harvard Medical School and becoming a cardiologist. The writing is fluent, easy to read and understand. The sequence of events is realistic, emotionally moving, spiritually touching, heart-warming, and thought provoking. The book illustrates . . . how one must have faith in order to walk through life's winding path." (Printed book: $14.95; PDF eBook: $8.95; together: $22.95; commercial eBook reader version: $9.99.)

12 Parables, by Wayne Faust – Timeless Christian stories about doubt, fear, change, grief, and more. Using tight, entertaining prose, professional musician and comedy performer Wayne Faust manages to deal with difficult concepts in a simple, straightforward way. These are stories you can read aloud over and over—to your spouse, your family, or in a group setting. Packed with emotion and just enough mystery to keep you wondering, while providing lots of points to ponder and discuss when you're through, these stories relate the gospel in the tradition of the greatest speaker of parables the world has ever known, who appears in them often. (Printed book: $14.95; PDF eBook: $8.95; together: $22.95; commercial eBook reader version: $9.99.)

The Answer is Always "Jesus," by Aram Haroutunian, who gave children's sermons for 15 years at a large church in Golden, Colorado—well over 500 in all. This book contains 74 of his most unforgettable presentations—due to the children's responses. Pastors, homeschoolers, parents who often lead family  devotions, or other storytellers will find these stories, along with comments about props and how to prepare and present them, an invaluable asset in reconnecting with the simplest, most profound truths of Scripture, and then to envision how best to communicate these so even a child can understand them.(Printed book: $12.95; PDF eBook: $8.95; together: $19.95; commercial eBook reader version: $9.99.)

New FROM HEALTHY LIFE PRESS
CHECK WEBSITE FOR DETAILS

The Secret of Singing Springs, by Monte Swan. One Colorado family's treasure-hunting adventure along the trail of Jesse James.

I AM – Transformed in Him, by Diana Burg and Kim Tapfer, a meditative women's Bible study of the I AM statements of Christ.

Nature-God's Second Book, by Elvy Rolle, who discovered true healing through immersing herself in God's beautiful Creation. In this full-color book (print/ePub) she shares her insights.

Handbook of Faith by Rev. Warren C. Biebel Jr. – The *New York Times World 2011 Almanac* claimed that there are 2 billion, 200 thousand Christians in the world, with "Christians" being defined as "followers of Christ." The original 12 followers of Christ changed the world; indeed, they changed the history of the world. So this author, a pastor with over 60 years' experience, poses and answers this logical question: "If there are so many 'Christians' on this planet, why are they so relatively ineffective in serving the One they claim to follow?" Answer: Because, unlike Him, they do not know and trust the Scriptures, implicitly. This little volume will help you do that. (Printed book: $8.95; PDF eBook: $6.95; together: $13.95; commercial eBook reader version: $8.95.)

Pieces of My Heart, by David L. Wood – Eighty-two lessons from normal everyday life. David's hope is that these stories will spark thoughts about God's constant involvement and intervention in our lives and stir a sense of how much He cares about every detail that is important to us. The piece missing represents his son, Daniel, who died in a fire shortly before his first birthday. (Printed book: $16.95; PDF eBook: $8.95; Set: $24.95; commercial eBook version: $9.99.)

PLEASE NOTE: Prices of resources listed in this catalog may have changed since these pages were printed. Current prices are available at:
www.healthylifepress.com.

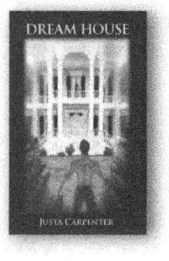

Dream House by Justa Carpenter – Written by a New England builder of several hundred homes, the idea for this book came to him one day as he was driving that came to him one day as was driving from one job site to another. He pulled over and recorded it so he would remember it, and now you will remember it, too, if you believe, as he does, that ". . . He who has begun a good work in you will complete it until the day of Jesus Christ." (Printed book: $8.95; PDF eBook: $6.95; Set: $13.95; commercial eBook reader version: $8.95.)

A Simply Homemade Clean, by homesteader Lisa Barthuly – "Somewhere along the path, it seems we've lost our gumption, the desire to make things ourselves," says the author. "Gone are the days of 'do it yourself.' Really . . . why bother? There are a slew of retailers just waiting for us with anything

and everything we could need; packaged up all pretty, with no thought or effort required. It is the manifestation of 'progress' . . . right?" I don't buy that!" Instead, Lisa describes how to make safe and effective cleansers for home, laundry, and body right in your own home. This saves money and avoids exposure to harmful chemicals often found in commercially produced cleansers. (Printed book: $12.99; PDF eBook: $6.95; Set: $14.95; commercial eBook reader version: $8.95.)

Unless otherwise noted on the site itself, shipping is free for all products purchased through www.healthylifepress.com.

RECOMMENDED RESOURCES – PRO-LIFE DVD SERIES

SEE WWW.HEALTHYLIFEPRESS.COM (SELECT "DVD")
FOR TRAILERS AND SPECIAL COMBINATION PRICING

EYEWITNESS 2 (PUBLIC SCHOOL VERSION) – This DVD has been used in many public schools. It is a fascinating journey through 38 weeks of pregnancy, showing developing babies via cutting edge digital ultrasound technology. Separate chapters allow viewing distinct segments individually. (List Price: $34.95; Sale Price: $24.95.)

WINDOW TO THE WOMB (2 DVD DISC SET) Disc 1: Ian Donald (1910-1987) "A Prophetic Legacy;" Disc 2: "A Journey from Death To Life" (50 min) – Includes history of sonography and its increasing impact against abortion—more than 80% of expectant parents who "see" 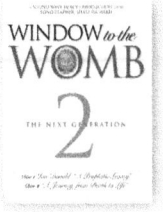 their developing baby choose for life. Perfect for counseling and education in Pregnancy Centers, Christian schools, homeschools, and churches. (List: $49.95; Sale: $34.95.)

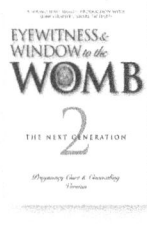

WINDOW TO THE WOMB (PREGNANCY CARE & COUNSELING VERSION) – Facts about fetal development, abortion complications, post-abortion syndrome, and healing. Separate chapters allow selection of specialized presentations to accommodate the needs and time constraints of their situations. (List: $34.95; Sale: $24.95.)

RECOMMENDED RESOURCES – BOOKS

If God Is So Good, Why Do I Hurt So Bad?, by David B. Biebel, DMin – In this best-selling classic (over 200,000 copies in print worldwide, in five languages) on the subject of loss and renewal, first published in 1989, the author comes alongside people in pain, and shows the way through and beyond it, to joy again. This book has proven helpful to those who are struggling and to those who wish to understand and help. Revised and re-released July 2010. (Printed book: $12.95; PDF eBook: $8.95; Set: $19.95.)

52 Ways to Feel Great Today, by David B. Biebel, DMin, James E. Dill, MD, and Bobbie Dill, RN **– Increase Your Vitality, Improve your Outlook.** Simple, fun, inexpensive things you can do to increase your vitality and improve your outlook. Why live an "ordinary" life when you could be experiencing the extraordinary?

Don't settle for good enough when "great" is such a short stretch away. Make today great! (Printed book: $14.99.)

The A to Z Guide To Healthier Living, by David B. Biebel, DMin, James E. Dill, MD, and Bobbie Dill, RN – You'll find great info on: avoiding fad diets, being kind to your GI tract, building healthy bones, finding contentment, getting a good night's sleep, keeping your relationships strong, simplifying your life, staying creative, and much more. (Printed book: 12.99; commercial eBook versions: $8.99.)

New Light on Depression, a CBA Gold Medallion winner, by David B. Biebel, DMin, and Harold Koenig, MD – The most exhaustive Christian resource on a subject that is more common than we might wish. Hope for those with depression and help for those who love them. (Printed book: $15.00.)

VOWS, a Romantic novel by F.F. Whitestone – When the police cruiser pulled up to the curb outside, Faith Framingham's heart skipped a beat, for she could see that Chuck, who should have been driving, was not in the vehicle. Chuck's partner, Sandy, stepped out slowly. Sandy's pursed lips and ashen face spoke

volumes. Faith waited by the front door, her hands clasped tightly, to counter the fact that her mind was already reeling. "Love never fails." A compelling story. (Printed book: $12.99; full color PDF eBook: $9.99. Combination, only from publisher: $19.99. Other eReader options: BN.com and Amazon.com.)

Our God Given Senses, by Gary A. Burlingame – Did you know humans have NINE senses? The Bible draws on these senses to reveal spiritual truth. We are to taste and see that the Lord is a good. We are to carry the fragrance of Christ. Our faith is produced upon hearing. Jesus asked Thomas to touch him. God created us for a sensory experience and that is what you will find in this book. (Printed book: $12.99; full color PDF eBook: $9.99; together: $19.99, direct from publisher; other eReader options: BN.com and Amazon.com. Available Spring 2013.)

God Loves You Circle, by Michelle John-son – Daily inspiration for your deeper walk with Christ. This collection of short stories of Christian living will make you laugh, make you cry, but most of all make you contemplate–the meaning and value of walking with the Master moment-by-moment, day-by-day. (Full-color printed book: $17.95, PDF eBook: $9.99; set $24.95, direct from publisher; eBook versions: $9.99, at eChristian.com; Amazon.com; BN.com.)

ABOUT HEALTHY LIFE PRESS

Healthy Life Press was founded with a primary goal of helping previously unpublished authors to get their works to market, and to reissue wor-thy, previously published works that were no longer available. Our mission is to help people toward optimal vitality by providing resources promoting physical, emotional, spiritual, and re-lational health as viewed from a Christian per-spective. We see health as a verb, and achieving optimal health as a process—a crucial process for followers of Christ if we are to love the Lord with all our heart, soul, mind, AND strength, and our neighbors as ourselves—for as long as He leaves us here. We are a collaborative and cooperative small Christian publisher. We share the costs, we share the proceeds.

For information about publishing with us, e-mail: <u>info@healthylifepress.com</u>.

www.ingramcontent.com/pod-product-compliance
Lightning Source LLC
Chambersburg PA
CBHW061253040426
42444CB00010B/2375